THE
CHERNOBYL
DISASTER

A BRIEF HISTORY FROM BEGINNING TO END

HISTORY HUB

Bonus Downloads

*Get Free Books with **<u>Any Purchase</u>** History Shorts*

Every purchase comes with a FREE download!

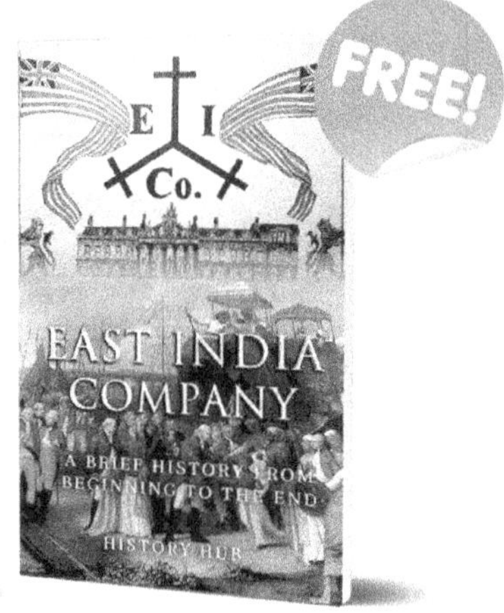

The Chernobyl Disaster

A Brief History from Beginning to the End

History Shorts

CONTENTS

Chapter One
Introduction

On 26 April 1986, a disaster occurred at the reactor No. 4 in the Chernobyl Nuclear Power Plant, situated near Pripyat, a city in the north of the Ukraine. It is one of the only two atomic power emergencies rated at the maximum severity level of 7. This is one of the ratings issued by the "International Nuclear Event Scale." The other nuclear disaster was in 2011 in Fukushima, Japan. The preliminary disaster response and the later rounds of environmental decontamination consisted of 500,000 experts and clean-up crew and cost more than a substantial 18 billion roubles.

The Chernobyl disaster was caused by a defective reactor run by poorly trained staff. This can be seen as a direct outcome of isolation because of the Cold War and the absence of a culture of safety.

The ensuing explosion, which was largely composed of steam, followed by fire, discharged more than 5% of the highly radioactive reactor core into the atmosphere and the surrounding habitat. Radioactive materials were released into numerous areas in Europe.

Two Chernobyl factory employees perished owing to the effects of the explosion on the night of the disaster. Another 28 people were deceased within a period of a couple of weeks because of their radiation exposure. Two hundred and thirty-seven people were initially thought to have acute radiation syndrome (ARS), and this was confirmed in 134 cases. After the initial twenty-eight deaths, nineteen more workers lost their lives between 1987 and 2004, however, their deaths cannot be attributed with certainty to radiation exposure. No one offsite experienced the effects of acute radiation syndrome. A study on the effects of radiation by The United Nations Scientific Committee came to a conclusion that, regardless of about 5,000 cancers of the thyroid, which resulted in 15 fatalities, "there is no evidence of a major public health impact attributable to radiation exposure 20 years after the accident." This is certainly an interesting take on the subject, particularly since a notable number of these cancers were in patients who had been children at the time and were likely to be susceptible to the intake of high levels of radioactive iodine.

Big areas of Ukraine, Belarus, and Russia suffered varying degrees of contamination. As an outcome of the disaster, there was a mass evacuation of more than 350 thousand people, but there is ongoing resettlement of these areas.

On 24 February 2022, Ukraine notified the International Atomic Energy Agency (IAEA) that Putin's Russian troops had managed to take control of all buildings and facilities at the Chernobyl nuclear plant. On 9 March 2022, the Chernobyl nuclear facility was isolated from the grid. While it had been a significant electricity supplier, the IAEA asserted that it saw no considerable safety impact due to this.

The Chernobyl disaster led to vital changes in the culture of nuclear safety cooperation between East and West even before the Soviet Union ended. Former President Mikhail Gorbachev intimated that the Chernobyl disaster was a more significant component of the Soviet Union's collapse than his policy of liberal reform, Perestroika.

Chapter Two
Chernobyl – The Background

The city of Chernobyl is now a largely abandoned area because of the nuclear power leak of 1986, but it was once a small but thriving place with 14,000 residents. About 1000 people have been repatriated since 1986. Its name is written as Chornobyl in Russian. It's situated 90 km (60 miles) to the north of Kyiv, the capital of Ukraine.

The first mention of "Czernobol" was from the 2nd century AD on Ptolemy's map. Chernobyl was later used as a hunting lodge belonging to the Grand Prince of Kyiv, Rurik Rostislavich in 1193. In 1362, it belonged to the Grand duchy of Lithuania and had its own castle, which was ruined twice in 1473 and 82. The city has changed hands many times during its history. In 1552, it boasted 196 buildings and more than 1300 residents and was quite a center for trade and artisans. In 1566, it was given to Filon Kmita, a royal cavalry captain, as a fiefdom. After the Union of Lublin, it was transferred as Crown lands to the Polish kingdom. In the 1500s, a Jewish community moved into the city, and in 1626, a monastery, which is now defunct, was established. There was a great deal of religious repression throughout this period. Eastern Orthodox Christians were severely repressed and forced to convert to the Ruthenian Church by the Polish administration. By the late 1700's Chernobyl was a key center for Hasidic Judaism, which is an ultra-conservative sect founded by the high rabbi, Menachem Nachum Twersky. By the mid-1700s, a series of dramatic peasant riots had to be suppressed by an army of Hussars. In 1793, the Russian Empire annexed Chernobyl. The city was also subjected to Jewish repression and massacres called pogroms in the early 1900s. The Black Hundreds, a Russian monarchist anti-nationalist, right-wing group, was responsible for these atrocities. The Germans occupied Chernobyl during WW1, and its entire Jewish community was massacred during the Holocaust. Vladimir Putin later used this event as a justification for accusing the Ukrainian government of being Nazi during the war of 2022.

The Ukrainians and Bolsheviks battled to keep control over the city during the Polish-Soviet struggle of 1919–20. Chernobyl was first captured by the Polish Army and subsequently by the Red Army cavalry. After 1921, it was officially incorporated into Ukraine.

Between 1929 and 1933, Chernobyl endured many murders during Stalin's collectivization crusade. It was also impacted on by the dreadful Holodomor famine, which was caused by Stalin's cruel economic policies. The Polish and German Chernobyl community was taken to Kazakhstan in 1936 during Stalin's infamous Frontier Clearances.

According to populartimelines.com, "in 1972, the Duga-1 radio receiver, part of the larger Duga over-the-horizon radar array, began construction 11 km (6.8 mi) west-northwest of Chernobyl." The Duga-1 radio receiver was developed as part of an "anti-ballistic missile early warning radar network."

On 15 August 1972, building began on what would become the Vladimir Ilyich Lenin Nuclear Power Plant, more commonly known as the Chernobyl Nuclear Power Plant. It was constructed next to the city of Pripyat, a "atomograd" founded on February 4, 1970. An atomograd city was designed to supply the nuclear power plant with a skilled labor force, and it was constructed for this purpose. The decision to build the power plant in the Ukrainian SSR was recommended by the State Planning Committee and was later authorized by the Central Committee of the Communist Party of the Soviet Union. It was the country's first attempt at building a nuclear power facility. The station consisted of four reactors, each one of which could produce 1,000 megawatts of electricity.

Chernobyl was the site of the first nuclear power plant in Ukraine. Located 15 km north of the city of Chernobyl, it was opened in 1977. On 5 May 1986, Chernobyl was evacuated after the catastrophic nuclear fallout when part of the plant exploded. This was the largest atomic disaster ever recorded. The residents of Chernobyl and the residents of nearby Pripyat, which had been built for the nuclear plants' workforce, were moved to the new city of Slavutych. To this day, most people have not returned to Chernobyl, which has fewer than 1000 residents.

1991 to present Independent Ukraine

With the abolishment of the Soviet Union in 1991, Chernobyl stayed part of Ukraine as part of the Chernobyl Exclusion Zone that the country took over from the Union.

Chapter Three
Chernobyl — What caused the disaster?

The Chernobyl disaster of 1986 was caused by a damaged reactor with a flawed design that was operated by poorly trained staff. The resulting vapor eruption and fires released at least 5% of the radioactive reactor core into the atmosphere, with a significant amount of radioactive material fallout reaching numerous parts of Europe.

The April 1986 Chernobyl disaster in Ukraine was a direct outcome of Cold War isolation and the ensuing lack of any culture of safety. The accident devastated the Chernobyl 4 nuclear reactor. One person died immediately, and a second succumbed to injuries soon after. Thirty firemen and plant operators died within a three-month period, and there were several deaths after this. Acute radiation syndrome (ARS) was diagnosed in more than 200 people on-site and on those involved in cleaning up. It was reported that twenty-eight people died of ARS some weeks after the disaster, and another nineteen people were killed between 1987 and 2004. People off-site were apparently not affected by acute radiation, although a significant number of thyroid cancers over the years were almost definitely linked to Chernobyl. Big areas in Belarus, Ukraine, Russia and areas in other parts of Europe were also affected by the fallout.

The 1986 Chernobyl disaster occurred just before a routine shutdown on 26 April. The crew in charge of the reactor at the Chernobyl 4 core decided to run a test to ascertain how long the turbines would be able to spin and provide power to the major circulating pumps in the event of an electrical power supply outage or cut-off. When this test had been attempted previously, the power coming from the turbine ran low too quickly, so they wanted to test new designs for voltage regulators. A sequence of operator errors, including a mistake in disabling the mechanisms for automatic closedown, occurred during the attempted test on 26 April. Unfortunately, by the time the plant operator had made the move to close down the reactor, it was in a very unstable state. A design fault in the control rods created a terrible power surge when they were placed into the reactor. The interaction of combining extremely hot fuel with cool water caused fuel breakdown, fast steam production, and a significant pressure increase. The strange design of the reactor created considerable damage to three of four nuclear fuel assemblies and resulted in the reactor being destroyed. This high pressure meant that the 1000-ton cover plate on the reactor became detached. It burst open the fuel channels and jammed all control rods, which were still in the halfway position, and strong steam filled the whole core. This was fed by water which had filled the core because of the bursting of the circuit which ran the emergency cooling. This caused a massive steam explosion that released nuclear fission by-products into the atmosphere.

A few seconds later, another explosion threw fragments and hot graphite out from the fuel channels. There is some argument among experts about the nature of the second explosion. Still, it was very likely to have arisen because of the release of hydrogen produced from the reaction of zirconium and steam. Two employees died instantly because of these explosions. The graphite (about 25% of the available 1,200 tonnes was estimated to have escaped) and the fuel became incandescent, much like lava, and this started a series of fires. This caused the major release of radioactive fallout into the areas beyond the reactor. Attempts were made to cool the reactor by pumping water into it, but the danger of flooding in reactors 1 and 2 stopped them. From day one until day ten, 5,000 tons of materials like clay, lead, boron, sand, and dolomite were dropped by helicopters onto the burning core to try to put out the fire and reduce the escape of radiation.

While it's true that the operators put their plant in a dangerous situation by allowing it to become unstable, they did not violate any operating principles because such principles and safety guidelines had never been put in place in the first place. This was an unusual occurrence and the only time in history where a commercial nuclear power plant was responsible for radiation deaths and injuries. Former Russian president Mikhail Gorbachev was of the opinion that the Chernobyl accident was a more significant factor in the fall of the Soviet Union than his strategy of liberal reform policy called Perestroika.

Chapter Four
Interesting Facts about Chernobyl

Chernobyl never ceases to fascinate. An award-winning miniseries was written about it, and it's a popular tourist destination.

The official reports of Chernobyl-related deaths are very modest. Twenty-nine deaths in a short period, and years later, a report of some fifteen children dying of thyroid cancer potentially because of exposure to radiation poisoning. Estimates on future deaths are also rather low. Chernobyl-induced cancers by 2065 are estimated to total only 41,000 compared to hundreds of millions of other cancers. However, actual numbers might be a lot higher than the reported ones. There are no public records on Chernobyl-related fatalities in Ukraine, Belarus, and Russia, but other figures tell a different story. The Ukrainian government claimed in 2016 that nearly 2 million Ukrainians were victims of Chernobyl, and that they paid compensation to 350,000 spouses of those who had died of health problems related to the disaster. These figures don't even factor in Belarus and Russia, where the estimated Chernobyl-related health problems are in the thousands. It's fairly obvious that the Chernobyl death records were intentionally underreported for political reasons.

The area of the disaster reached much further than just the regions mentioned. The whole of Europe faced some fallout, and even today, some British farmers face restrictions on the sale of their meat. Recently, radioactive mushrooms from Belarus were turned back in France, and some contaminated berries are often sold in Europe from Ukraine.

Chernobyl is frequently described as the most terrible nuclear catastrophe in the history of humankind, and it certainly was ranked as a Level 7 disaster, the worst ranking level. Nonetheless, while Chernobyl discharged the highest amount of radioactivity at any one time for an accident, not for an intentional act of war, other nuclear incidents released way more radioactive isotopes into the environment. Just as an example, Chernobyl released about 45 million curies of radioactive iodine. This is known to cause thyroid cancer. In comparison, US and Soviet bomb tests between 1945 and 1962 released about 20 billions of these radioactive isotypes.

Chernobyl now provides an enduring portrayal of Soviet scientists and state officials as uniquely useless at doing their jobs. Grigori Mednedev wrote these words in his book, The Truth about Chernobyl: "The Ferris wheel left in the city's decaying amusement park still stands testament to the folly of the corrupt, paranoid, and inept Soviet system."

In fact, the Soviet reaction to the catastrophe was remarkable. The Soviets are frequently condemned for waiting some days to notify the public of a disaster. Hiding it meant that neighboring nations, like Poland, would not receive defensive prophylactic iodine in time. Soviet authorities did, however, act swiftly to protect their own nationals from nuclear fallout. Within 36 hours, 50,000 residents of Pripyat were relocated, and plans for an exclusion zone were put into play.

There was also an impressive medical response, as identified by a crew of American doctors who helped Soviet doctors to deal with the injured firefighters and power plant operators at the Hospital No 6 in Moscow. The American doctors were very impressed by how accurately the Soviet doctors could estimate radiation dosages by examining a patient's vital signs. They also remarked on the extraordinary range of Soviet therapies for radiation poisoning that were foreign to Western doctors. Of the 19 patients who underwent risky liver and bone marrow transplants proposed by the American team, only one survived. Meanwhile, more patients with potentially fatal radiation doses survived Soviet doctors' therapies, which is a testament to their skills and possibly to their experience with treating radiation damage.

Acute Radiation Syndrome (ARS) is also known as radiation sickness. It is an acute illness caused by severe exposure to radiation usually over a few minutes. The main cause of ARS is the eradication or reduction of undeveloped parenchymal stem cells in various tissues of the body. People who suffered from ARS were the Hiroshima and Nagasaki survivors of the atomic bomb assault by the USA, the firefighters who were the first responders to the explosion in the Chernobyl Nuclear Power Plant, and even accidental exposure to the irradiators, which caused sterilization.

Because of the dangerous effects of radiation caused by the Chernobyl explosion, the Soviet Union made a wide exclusion zone with a 30-km radius. It was later expanded to 4,143 sq km in an attempt to curtail any efforts at repopulation of the intensely radiated region beyond the immediate zone.

Chapter Five
Disastrous Radiation Effects

While people suffered from the terrible effects of radiation poisoning, the entire environment was affected by the nuclear fallout. Radiation has the most severe effects on bone marrow, the GI tract, the central nervous system, and the cardiac system. The impact on these body systems is usually so severe that death occurs in a matter of days or weeks.

ARS has four stages:

- Prodromal, which occurs minutes after exposure and includes symptoms of diarrhea and vomiting.

- Latent, where the patient looks and feels quite healthy for a few hours or even weeks.

- Manifest, which is where all or some of the typical symptoms of ARS are experienced.

- Recovery or Death. If death does occur, it's likely to be within a few months after the incident.

Section 1: The animals of Chernobyl

Strangely enough, animals are thriving in the exclusion zone around Chernobyl. Initially, animals would have been exposed to radiation as people were and would have suffered similar symptoms and consequences. Still, once the exclusion zone was established, animals began to trickle back. Ironically, it appears that although radiation is bad for animals, its effects on people are worse. Scientific studies have found significant levels of radiation and birth and other defects in small animals like mice and birds, but it's harder to gauge the effects on large mammals like elk, boar, and wolves.

Animal population in the exclusion zone is growing dramatically. Przewalski's horse or the Mongolian wild horse, an endangered species originally common to the Central Asian steppes, has been reintroduced. Exotic animals like lynx have been spotted. There is also a huge feral dog population. Chernobyl's feral dogs are the ancestors of those kept as pets before the disaster. They seldom live longer than four years but that's largely because of the harsh cold winters and not an effect of prolonged radiation exposure. Care groups are trying to protect the dogs, and some decontaminated ones are being rehomed.

Scientists are torn on the safety of animals in the exclusion zone. Their numbers are growing, but they are radioactive. Animals far from the site of the disaster have also shown effects. In Germany, the wild boar population is mildly radioactive. There is also the risk of contamination of healthy species by migratory animals leaving the exclusion zone, and no one is sure how great the trouble is.

Section 2: The ecosystem of Chernobyl

The Chernobyl disaster, as you are aware, created severe radiation toxicity and environmental contamination. Between 50 and 185 million curies (which is a unit of radioactivity named after Pierre Curie) of radionuclides were freed into the environment. Vast acres of farmland and forest were exposed and contaminated. Livestock and wild animals were born with deformities, and humans were affected by long-term negative health effects.

The Red Forest, translated from Rudyi Lis, literally means ginger-colored forest. It's a ten-square-kilometer zone surrounding the Chernobyl Power Plant. It's within the xclusion one and can be found in Polesia. Its name, "Red Forest," arises from the gingerish color of the pine trees, which died after absorbing extreme levels of ionizing radiation released during the Chernobyl nuclear explosion. During the cleanup of the disaster, the Red Forest was bulldozed to the ground and buried deeply in "waste graveyards" to try and reduce the airborne spread of contagion. Nonetheless, this forest site is one of the most tainted and contaminated places in the world.

Chapter Six
The Soviet Union and Ukraine

It's interesting to ask the question why Russia was even in Ukraine building nuclear power plants in the first place. Ukraine, at that stage, belonged to Russia and not for the first time in its history either. Ukraine and Russia have a long history of similarities and relationships in all areas like faith, economics, culture, and history.

Section 1: Russian-Ukraine Links

Experts describe the two countries as being "joined at the hip." They share a common language. The Russian media has always been popular in Ukraine, although the war of 2022 has gone a long way to sour that. There are extensive family ties. Many Ukrainians have worked in Russia over the generations, and Russians have always invested heavily in Ukraine. These ties historically date back to the time prior to the Soviet Union and even to the time before the Russian empire that arose in the 1700s.

Historians consider Ukraine to be the home of the area's Orthodox Christianity. Ukraine became a part of the Russian empire and the Soviet

Famine hit Ukraine in 1932–1933, and Soviet ruler Joseph Stalin was largely to blame. The aftermath of the Chernobyl tragedy was felt most severely throughout the Soviet countries.

Undoubtedly, the events will reverberate in people's minds for quite some time. In 1991, Ukraine was one of the first Soviet republics to overwhelmingly support separation from the Soviet Union through a ballot. The Soviet Union crumbled soon thereafter.

Those occurrences unquestionably will resonate in public memory for years to come. Ukraine was one of the initial Soviet republics to vote for independence from the Soviet Union which it did with an overwhelming majority in 1991. The Soviet Union collapsed soon thereafter.

Are You Enjoying Reading?

As an independent publisher

with a tiny marketing budget

we rely on readers, like you.

If you're receiving help from this book,

would you please take a moment to write a brief review?

We really appreciate it.

Chapter Seven
The Melting of the Iron Curtain and other Lessons from Chernobyl

The Ukrainian and Russian people and the world generally learned some important safety lessons from the Chernobyl disaster.

Section 1: The Melting of the Iron Curtain

The Chernobyl disaster put the Soviet Union on the spot. The disaster was first picked up by nuclear detection devices in Sweden. Within days, people were told not to eat raw salad or vegetables in Germany, Switzerland, UK, and other European countries. Animals have also been affected in all these areas. People in neighboring countries lost a lot of money when they could not sell their livestock or fresh produce. The Soviet Union could not hide from the consequences of its error. Along with the fact that the disaster led to some melting of the impenetrable Iron Curtain, the Russians found they could not hide all their actions from the wider world. In matters of nuclear disasters, they needed to be more transparent and compliant, and there were significant other effects on international atomic safety.

Section 2: Safety first

After the Chernobyl disaster, the main industry changes concerned reactor safety, particularly among Eastern European countries. This guided how the US dealt with the Three Mile Island disaster of 1979, which had a major influence on Western reactor design and operating protocols. While the radioactivity was contained, and there were no casualties, the Three Mile Island plant's reactor was destroyed, and it had given the West a scare. No one in the West had any illusions concerning the safety of Soviet reactor designs in those early days but some of the lessons learned have been applied to Western nuclear plants.

Necessarily, the security and safety of all Soviet-designed nuclear reactors have been vastly refined. This is owing largely to the growth of a culture of security and safety encouraged by improved teamwork between Western and Eastern powers and significant investment in developing safer reactors. Improvements have been brought about to beat any deficiencies in all Russian RBMK reactors that are still in operation. In these reactors, initially, the nuclear chain reaction and the output of power could intensify dangerously if the water intended for cooling was lost or became steam. This was different from most of the Western prototypes, and led to the runaway power surge that caused damage to Chernobyl 4.

All of these reactors have now been modified by alterations to the control rods, making them considerably more stable. The automatic mechanisms which shut down the reactor now perform faster, which reduces the chance of an accident. Inspection devices are also automated now. A repeat of the 1986 Chernobyl disaster is now practically impossible. Since 1989, more than 1,000 nuclear scientists and engineers from the previous Soviet Union have toured several Western atomic power plants and vice versa. Twinning arrangements between power plants have also helped to breach any distrust and ensure safety. All of this and the various bodies to which the ex-Soviet Union and Western countries belong keep information current and safety protocols up to date.

Chapter Eight
Chernobyl today

Amazingly, people are gradually moving back into areas affected by nuclear fallout. Belarus has just started huge projects to repatriate people into the Chernobyl fallout zones.

Section 1: The People who returned to Chernobyl before the Russian War of 2022

Chernobyl is still largely a ghost town, but people do live there now. The admin personnel and watch workers who still work there to monitor the plant live in a hotel. There are also two general stores.

In 2011, Chernobyl was declared an official tourist attraction and received high numbers of visitors. In 2015, the findings of an important scientific study indicated that the animal population of the exclusion zone was prospering, despite the contamination of the land. The study indicated that "data showed no evidence of a negative influence of radiation on mammal abundance." This certainly made people feel safer about returning.

Section 2: Life in modern Chernobyl

Social Resilience

In the period following the blast, around 1,200 people who had been evacuated made their way back to the exclusion zone. This was both illegal and hazardous, but many people chose to take the risk because they had a strong relationship with their land. They had survived Holodomor and Nazi devastation, and we're not convinced about the dangers of an unseen enemy. These people were defying the law and the guidance of investigators who considered the soil, livestock, food, and climate in the exclusion zone highly radioactive. Today, 100 people are still in the city, but others live close by, where the risks of radiation poisoning are much lower.

People moved into abandoned houses and set up their lives again. Part of the motivation behind moving into previously evacuated areas has been the political turmoil in Ukraine since 2014. The state of tension and upheaval resulted in the deaths of 10,000 people and the displacement of 2 million people more. Areas just outside the exclusion zone are becoming popular for those ousted by conflict seeking for a peaceful and cheap place to live. This creates social resilience as people recover a sense of normality after years of conflict. Of course, the War of 2022 has once again thrown the Ukrainian people into chaos.

Economic Resilience

Areas fringing the exclusion area have become a tempting alternative for entrepreneurs. Some of the exclusion areas are as close as 115 km to Ukraine's capital, Kyiv. This near proximity to the capital city, combined with the cheap cost of land, has made these regions popular for businessmen and women seeking reasonable property, such as vacant warehouses, to start up their businesses. To bolster economic resilience in tainted areas in Belarus, the authorities have provided tax exemptions, better healthcare, healthy food and water, and government-assisted programs to benefit economic rehabilitation.

Some people can work at the power plant, which is contained behind a steel shield to protect the 3,000 workers that still work at Chernobyl. An additional 2,000 workers, like guards, firemen, service staff, sentries, etc., work in the area on a strict 15 days off, 15 days on rotation. The government has built a solar plant on the site of the damaged nuclear plant. This is another drawcard for those who have returned to work and

live in the surrounding areas of Chernobyl.

Chapter Nine
Russia and Chernobyl 2022

During the 2022 Russian attack on Ukraine, Chernobyl was the site of the Battle of Chernobyl. Russian troops inhabited the city from 24 February to 2 April. After it was captured, radiation levels were reported to be rising.

Section 1: Why Russia went to War

Vladimir Putin declared the largest war in Europe since the end of World War Two with the rationale that contemporary Ukraine, which was leaning towards the West, was an ongoing danger, and Russia did not feel "safe to develop and exist." When he launched the onslaught on 24 February, he notified the Russian people that his objective was to "demilitarize and de-Nazify Ukraine." He aimed to safeguard people who had been subjected, according to him, to "eight years of bullying and genocide by Ukraine's government."

Putin's initial goal was to invade Ukraine and oust its government, finally stopping Ukraine's appetite for joining NATO. After months of blunders, he relinquished his plan to capture Kyiv and turned his sights to the east and south of Ukraine. Russia's leader, Putin, declined to call the assault an invasion. Moscow continues calling Europe's biggest war since WWII, a "special military operation." Russia is now condemned by the international community for executing war crimes. Some countries accuse him of genocide.

Thousands of Ukrainian and Russian people died, cities such as Mariupol were ruined, and more than 13 million people were forced to flee. We can ask the question: how will it finally end?

Section 2: Russian threat at Chernobyl

On 24 February, Ukraine notified the International Atomic Energy Agency (IAEA) that Russian troops had taken over all buildings and facilities at Chernobyl.

During the 2022 Russian attack on Ukraine, the Chernobyl Exclusion Zone was captured. This occurred on 24 February, the initial day of the invasion by the Russian soldiers. They infiltrated Ukrainian territory from its neighbor Belarus and occupied the whole region of the Chernobyl Nuclear Power Plant.

On 7 March, it was reported that 300 people, 200 security guards, and 100 plant workers were imprisoned, powerless to vacate the power plant. On 31 March, however, it was noted that the majority of the Russian armies invading the area had relinquished control and turned their attention to Eastern Ukraine. On 9 March, the Chernobyl nuclear power plant was separated from the Ukraine electricity grid.

Radiation rates rose during the Russian attack on Chernobyl, which caused significant alarm. Still, in the end, it was decided by the nuclear authorities that the rising radiation was probably due to "disturbance of the top layer of soil from the movement of a large number of heavy military machinery through the exclusion zone."

There was no real threat to safety, but it stressed an already stressed world. While nuclear power is considered to be a good thing under the right supervision, the Russians were not trusted to offer that protection particularly with the ongoing undertone and threat of using nuclear weapons, potentially turning the struggle to suppress Ukraine into WWIII.

Chapter Ten
Chernobyl and Dark Tourism

Auschwitz, Alcatraz, and Chernobyl are some of the many sites which offer a tourist experience known as dark tourism.

People like to visit places where others have suffered and died gruesome deaths, and Chernobyl is no exception. Two million people annually visit Auschwitz, while three hundred thousand enjoy visiting Robben Island to experience what it must have been like to be a prisoner of the Apartheid government. Chernobyl boasts 10,000 visitors a year. However, Covid and the Russian war will obviously have dented those figures significantly.

Some dark tourism sites might wish to shock or horrify, but others might offer a place for people to remember loved ones or fellow citizens lost in these places. The leader of a Jewish community that traced its roots back to the Hasidic community hundreds of years before has this to say, "We go there to [Chernobyl] to sing songs, light candles, and say psalms. It's a very special and emotional part of the trip." He had taken many groups to visit the Old Synagogue and graves, avoiding the main tourist attractions like the abandoned school, the old swimming pool and memorial sites.

Tourists first began thronging to Chernobyl about ten years ago, when enthusiasts of the video game S.T.A.L.K.E.R. wished to see the nuclear apocalypse that they had explored in virtual reality. Next came those tourists, scientists, and explorers whose interest was awakened when a giant steel dome was done over the damaged reactor in 2016.

After HBO's Chernobyl miniseries was aired, tourism companies were delighted with a huge increase in visitors to the abandoned area. A standard tour is described in a tourist leaflet that promises "innovative Chernobyl trips," which are interesting and exciting, offering not only an in-depth look into the disaster itself but broad explanations about nuclear disasters, radiation contamination, and survival of a radiation episode. "We must give this territory of Ukraine a new life," President Volodymyr Zelensky had said before the war tore any hopes of normal living away in 2022.

Although tourist dollars are a great temptation, scientists are a bit skeptical. The ground is still covered with a lingering coat of plutonium and other radionuclides, which are radiation-emitting atoms. These could present potentially severe health hazards to those who touch or eat them. Some regions have additional radiation and are more hazardous than others. As one expert puts it, "Even though the accident occurred over 33 years ago, it remains one of the most radiologically contaminated places on earth." Visitors are advised to wear shoes and clothes they can throw away, wear a mask and gloves and avoid stirring up dust or touching plant material.

Unfortunately, in this age of over-tourism, many people will inevitably stir up dust or disturb radioactive plant material. This will increase the risks of inhaling radiation, and because it's such an insidious thing that might cause cell damage many years later, people just don't realize that they might well be changing their own futures for the worst.

Chapter Eleven
Conclusion

We can learn a great deal from the nuclear disaster at Chernobyl. Nuclear power could be very significant in a world that is forced to reduce reliance on fossil fuels, as it is largely classified as clean energy. Nuclear energy is not always described as clean energy, though, because of incidents like Chernobyl, which have given it a bad rap. Nonetheless, nuclear energy is a zero-emissions source of a very powerful form of clean energy. Through a reaction known as nuclear fission, uranium atoms are split to create energy. The heat produced by atomic fission consequently creates steam, which then drives a turbine that generates electricity.

Its advantages are many. It has none of the harmful byproducts produced by fossil fuels like carbon. Nuclear energy in the USA in 2020 reduced carbon emissions by so much that it equated to removing 100 million cars from our roads. It also requires only a small land footprint. Unlike wind and solar farms, which require huge tracts of land, a nuclear power plant is quite compact. Finally, it produces minimal waste. Used nuclear fuel is minimal, and the waste could be reprocessed if people wished to do so. It would be better than storing it.

The problem with nuclear energy is that it's usually safe, efficient, and effective, BUT if things go wrong either with the human or mechanical aspect of its production, one could have an unmitigated human and environmental tragedy of the scale or greater than Chernobyl.

Once again, it's up to human beings to use nuclear energy wisely, cautiously and responsibly to avoid dangerous consequences. The Chernobyl nuclear power plant has been decommissioned during the current Russian-Ukrainian war because as soon as circumstances change and a war situation occurs, a plant like Chernobyl is no longer safe. It becomes vulnerable, and that makes it a risk to the environment and human safety.

We can be hopeful, however, that the greener, up and coming generations will have a good look at nuclear power, and see if they can find a way to use it safely and sensibly for the benefit of mankind and for the safety of the environment before global warming becomes so catastrophic that there's no turning back.

Chapter Twelve
Discussion Question

Animals are better off exposed to radiation and left to thrive than living in the proximity of people. What's your take on this, considering the evidence of Chernobyl? Illustrate your answer.

Discussion Question

The Chernobyl disaster has captured the popular imagination. Why do people find disasters fascinating? Do you feel this is acceptable?

Discussion Question

Explain what happened to cause the nuclear explosion. How do you think it could have been prevented? What safety steps should have been put in place?

Discussion Question

What do you think of the Russian attack on Ukraine in 2022? Who's right? What do you think?

Discussion Question

What do you think of re-establishing people in an exclusion zone? Is it

morally defensible? Yes or no?

Discussion Question

Stalin's economic policies created a terrible famine in Ukraine. This was called the Holodomor famine, where millions of Ukrainians died. Should Russia pay reparations for this? What do you think?

Discussion Question

What are the signs and symptoms of acute radiation poisoning? What are

the long-term effects? Do you think the deaths were underreported?

Discussion Question

Chernobyl was an accidental disaster. Can you name others? What

nuclear disasters have occurred in the last 100 years?

Chapter Thirteen
Quiz Question

1. **True/False:** Russia was not responsible for the Chernobyl nuclear disaster. Chernobyl is in Ukraine. It's unjust to blame the Russians.

2. **True/False:** Feral dogs live in Chernobyl city and its surroundings. They are not long-lived because of radiation poisoning.

3. **True/False:** Human error caused the Chernobyl disaster. The technicians were inadequately trained. There were insufficient safety protocols in place.

4. **True/False:** The Holodomor was the name of the terrible famine which affected the Ukrainian people. It was intentionally inflicted on them. Stalin was the perpetrator.

5. **True/ False:** People hate going to Chernobyl. It is a dark and frightening place. They avoid it unless they have to go there on business.

6. **True/False:** The Chernobyl disaster helped to end the Soviet Union. It added to the dissatisfaction that the Ukrainians felt. They were among the first to vote to leave.

7. **True/False:** Radiation poisoning is a terrible disease. It affects major organs. It can cause a painful death.

8. **True/ False:** The Red Forest was so called because it was overrun by Russian soldiers. They were deployed to clean up after the accident. They camped in the forest.

Quiz Answer

1. False: Ukraine was part of the Soviet Union during the Chernobyl disaster. Poor planning by the Soviet Union was to blame.

2. False: The dogs are not badly impacted by radiation. The cold, harsh winters affect their life span.

3. True

4. True

5. False: Dark tourism is very popular now. Chernobyl is a popular tourist destination.

6. True

7. True

8. False: The Red Forest turned brownish red after Chernobyl. It happened because of radiation damage to pine trees. They were bulldozed and buried after.

Bibliography

Chapter 2: On 5 May 1986, Chernobyl was evacuated after the catastrophic nuclear fallout when part of the plant exploded. This was the largest atomic disaster ever recorded. (Pixabay)

Chapter 3: What Happened to Cause the Disaster?

The nuclear power plant as it looks today - The Chernobyl disaster of 1986 was caused by a damaged reactor with a flawed design that was operated by poorly trained staff. (Pixabay)

Chapter 5.1: The animals of Chernobyl

Strangely enough, animals are thriving in the exclusion zone around Chernobyl. Initially, animals would have been exposed to radiation as people were and would have suffered similar symptoms and consequences. Still, once the exclusion zone was established, animals began to trickle back. Ironically, it appears that although radiation is bad for animals, the effects of exposure on people is worse. (iStock)

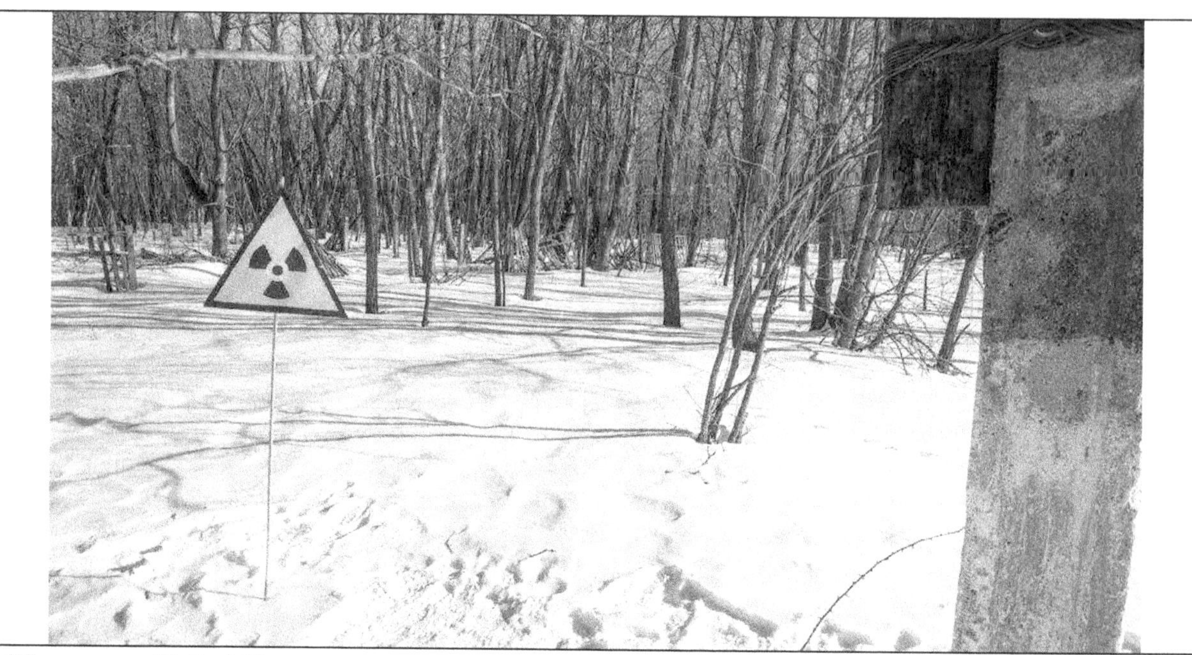# Chapter 5.2: The ecosystem of Chernobyl

The Chernobyl disaster, as you are aware, created severe radiation toxicity and environmental contamination. Between 50 and 185 million curies (which is a unit of radioactivity named after Pierre Curie) of radionuclides were freed into the environment. Vast acres of farmland and forest were exposed and contaminated. Livestock and wild animals were born with deformities, and humans were affected by long-term negative health effects. (Pixabay)

Chapter 7.1: Chernobyl, The Melting of the Iron Curtain, and the Fall of the Berlin Wall

The Chernobyl disaster put the Soviet Union on the spot. The disaster was first picked up by nuclear detection devices in Sweden. Within days people were told not to eat raw salad or vegetables in Germany, Switzerland, UK, and other European countries. Animals have been affected in all these areas. People in neighboring countries lost a lot of money when they could not sell their livestock or fresh produce. The Soviet Union could not hide from the consequences of its error. Along with the fact that the disaster led to some melting of the impenetrable Iron Curtain, the Russians found they could not hide all their actions from the wider world. The fall of the Berlin wall was pivotal in signaling the melting of the Iron Curtain. (Pixabay)

Chapter 8: Chernobyl Today

A monument entitled the "Monument to Those Who Saved the World" was erected to honor those men who lost their lives trying to put out the fire at Chernobyl. It is also dedicated to those men known as the

"Chernobyl Liquidators" who helped to clean up after the event. The monument stands in the town of Chernobyl in Ukraine. (Wiki Images)

Chapter 10: Chernobyl and Dark Tourism

People like to visit places where others have suffered and died gruesome deaths, and Chernobyl is no exception. Two million people annually visit Auschwitz, while three hundred thousand enjoy visiting Robben Island to experience what it must have been like to be a prisoner of the Apartheid government. Chernobyl boasts 10,000 visitors a year.

However, Covid and the Russian war will obviously have dented those

figures significantly. (Pixabay)

Bonus Downloads

*Get Free Books with **<u>Any Purchase</u>** History Shorts*

Every purchase comes with a FREE download!

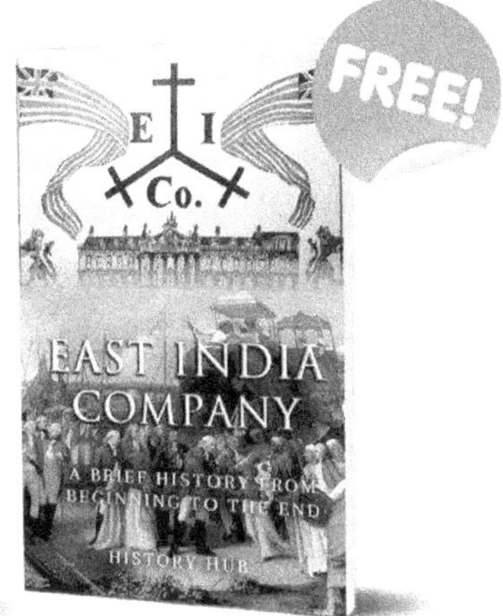

Thank You For Reading

As an independent publisher

with a tiny marketing budget

we rely on readers, like you.

If you're receiving help from this book,

would you please take a moment to write a brief review?

We really appreciate it.